D0513649

ULTIMATE DOG SHOW

Super Saviour

Colin Buchanan

G'day! I'm Colin. Welcome to Super Saviour!

It has been fun drawing and writing and singing and dressing up and doing all the things that go into making a book. I love making up songs about our wonderful God and His Word. Making a book is a special way to help us all think a little more about God's truths that I sing about in the songs from my CD called "Super Saviour".

Maybe you will sit with a grown-up and they'll read this book with you and you'll talk about what you've learnt together. Maybe you're old enough to read it on your own, or maybe you'll put on the CD that comes with the book and follow along. (I've put a few extra songs on the CD for you to enjoy!) Remember to look up the Bible readings and to pray, too!

Jesus is so wonderful and mighty and kind. What He did by His obedient life, His sin-smashing death and His death-crushing life is the most wonderful news for me and you and everyone. I pray that this book will help you to think about Him and believe in Him and follow Him, whether you are big or small, young or old, no matter where you are!

Oh, and don't forget to look for Super Little Colin - I've hidden him all over the place. Can you find him?

Colin

www.colinbuchanan.com.au

Super Saviour

Who can save the day and take our sins away and rescue us with mighty power? Jesus! He's the Super Saviour! He is strong enough to live His whole life in love and obedience to God. He is brave enough to face death on the cross, even though He didn't deserve it. He's kind enough to forgive sinners – even His own murderers! He's pure enough to be God's perfect sacrifice for sin. He's powerful enough to rise from the grave. Every one of us needs a Saviour to rescue us from sin, and there is only one death-crushing, sin-smashing Super Saviour. Who is it? Yes! Jesus!

Ze Baddest Sickness

It's no fun being sick is it? When you're sick you feel tired and sore and uncomfortable. When you're sick your body isn't working as it should and you can't do things like when you're healthy and well. Everyone gets a little bit sniffly and sneezily sick now and then. And sometimes people get very, very sick. All sickness is bad, but what do you think is the worst sickness of all? Sin! Sin is the worst sickness because we all are sick with sin and sin brings nothing but selfishness and sadness and strife and death. Sin makes us enemies of the holy God. He hates sin. Who can heal us from the horrible, deadly sickness of sin? Only Jesus! He defeats death, wins peace with God and promises us a happy and healthy, forever home with Him. Has Jesus healed you of the baddest sickness in the world?

Why is sin so BAD?

Nya Nya!

Sin says to God, "You're not the BOSS, I am!"

Sin kills sinners.

His dad died of the same thing... SIN...
John Doe

sin brings God's HOLY, EVERLASTING punishment.

Sin brings anger, hatred, fighting + strife. Got ya! Got ya!

me me me me me

Sin is a problem for EVERYONE.

QUITE BIG PILLS

CAUTION: ONE AT A TIME

Global Warning

In the Bible we read about how Jesus, after He was baptised by John, was tempted by Satan. Satan is God's enemy - a liar, a destroyer, a hater and harmer of everything good. He offered Jesus things that seemed good and used trickery. He told lies and he tried to get Jesus to sin. But Jesus trusted God, remembered His word and said "No!" to Satan and sin. Jesus knew that sin always wrecks lives and always makes things worse. He knew people needed to be warned about sin. Jesus is the only one with the power to save everyone who hears His warning, repents and believes.

READ THE BIBLE

SING 🎵
'Ze Baddest Sickness'
'Global warning'

LET'S PRAY!

Holy God, I know that, like every person, I'm sick with sin. I thank you that Jesus heals sinners and saves them from sin and the sadness and shame and sorrow that goes with it. What a merciful and mighty Saviour you are! Amen.

Only Jesus Can Make Sin Disappear

Have you ever seen a magician? Magicians are people who learn tricks that make people think, "Wow! How did they do that?" Magicians have secret ways to make the tricks work. They practise and practise to get the tricks right. A magician may make something look like it's disappeared but all they really do is hide it in a clever and tricky way so you can't see it. Sin is bad and deadly and people try to get rid of it and what it does. But, like the magician, we can't make sin disappear. We just hide it in clever and tricky ways. But God knows it's there and because He is holy He always punishes sin. I wonder, could anyone not just hide sin but really make sin and death disappear forever, so sinners like you and me could know God's love instead of His holy anger? Yes! Jesus can do that! Only Jesus can make sin disappear!

As far as the EAST is from the WEST so far has he removed our sin from us.
PSALM 103:12

The B-I-B-L-E

How can we know what God thinks, what He wants, what He likes, what He hates? Can we be His friend? Can He sort out this sad and sick world? Lots of people have made up answers to these questions that aren't true. They'll say things about God but they aren't right and they don't really know what God is like at all. Oh dear! How can we know what's true and what isn't? We need to listen to what God says about Himself – He always tells the truth!

But where does God speak to us? In the B-I-B-L-E! By His Holy Spirit, God guided men to write down His truth, to show us how holy and mighty and merciful He is. More than anything, we need to know the truth about God, so listen to God speak – listen to the Bible!

Can you find Colin in his old photographs?

From Everlasting – Psalm 90

Have you ever got up on a chilly day and put on an old jacket only to find that the sleeves are too short, it's hard to do up, tight and uncomfortable? Your jacket doesn't fit any more! What happened? The jacket didn't get smaller – you got...bigger! That's what happens as we grow until we're all grown up. We grow older and older and what happens when people get very, very old? Sadly, sooner or later, people die. But is God like that? No! The scriptures say that God is from everlasting to everlasting – He was forever there and He forever will be. All the time people are changing and getting older and dying. But God has been and always will be wonderfully and powerfully the same, without growing or changing or dying. That's what we mean when we say that God is eternal. And He loves with an eternal love that is from everlasting to everlasting.

everything in this picture won't be there some day...

What can you see?

".. for this world in it's present form is passing away"

1 CORINTHIANS 7:31

READ THE BIBLE
Psalm 90

SING
'From Everlasting'

LET'S PRAY!

Oh God, we live in this beginning-and-ending world and we so much need to know you and your everlasting love. Thank you for saving us through Jesus, your everlasting Son. Thank you for giving us your everlasting Spirit. You are amazing! Amen.

Have you ever had an argument with someone? I think we all do that sometimes. Have you ever lost a game or a race or a competition? I have. There always seems to be someone faster or smarter or better than me. Have you ever made a plan that ended up not happening? Yes! It may have been a bad plan, or someone stopped you or something went wrong and that was the end of your plan. Have you ever done just as you pleased? Yes! And very often doing just as we please ends up in sadness and badness. God is not like us. What He wants is always the best. He never loses. There is no one better than Him. His plans always happen. No one can stop God. He does whatever He pleases and it's always good. God is not a man. God is not like us. There is one triune God – Father, Spirit and Son. Triune means He's three persons but one God. No one is like Him! Who sits as heaven's King? GOD DOES!

READ THE BIBLE

SING ♪ 'God Does' 'Isaiah 46'

LET'S PRAY!

Great, Great, GREAT God, it is amazing that you are so good and powerful and right and true. Help me to remember that you do just as you please and that you are not a man but that you are God and there is no other. Amen.

Jesus Number 1

There are some mighty, mountains in the world. The highest mountain of all is called Mount Everest. It is very hard and very dangerous climbing Mt. Everest but some people have managed to get to the very top. But sometimes, when they finally get there, mist and clouds cover the whole mountain. All they can see is thick, grey fog. But... if the clouds part and the mist clears, suddenly they see a magnificent view of mountains and snow and valleys. That's when they know that they're standing on the very highest place in the world. Jesus rules this world but the mists of sin and unbelief can make us wonder, "Is Jesus really Number One?" We need to remember that one day Jesus will come in mighty power to blow away the mists of doubt and sin once and for all. On that day, everyone will see Jesus as He is – Number One, King of All! Will you trust and serve and honour Him now? Only those who believe in Jesus will be saved, to enjoy and marvel at the clear view of His goodness and greatness forever!

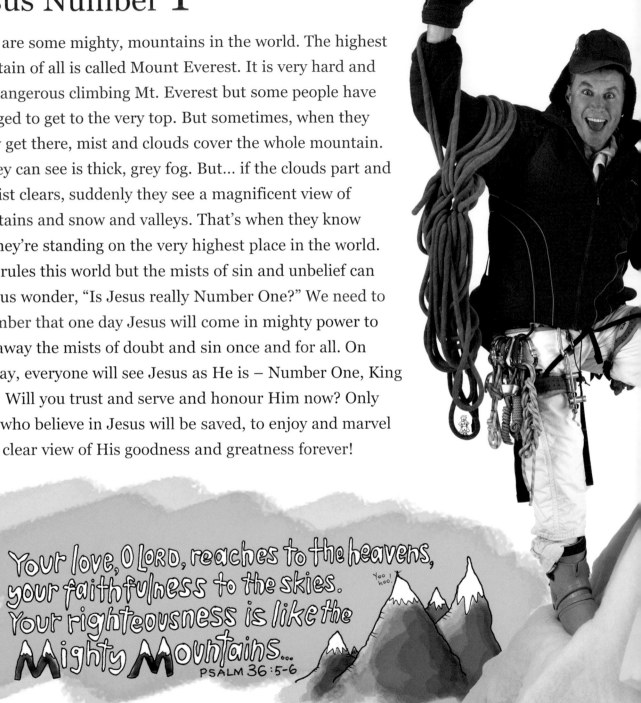

Your love, O LORD, reaches to the heavens, your faithfulness to the skies. Your righteousness is like the Mighty Mountains...

PSALM 36:5-6

Yoo! hoo.

Jesus number 1

FAIRY TALE FANCY DRESS

TEX
SLIM
BUDDY
KASEY

1ST CENTURION CATEGORY

ULTIMATE DOG SHOW

COUNTRY MUSIC

TALENT RADAR

Ya yah yee yodel haw haw giddy up

ART SHOW
BEST PAINTER MAY WIN!!!

WHO GETS THE PRIZE?

Can you match the winner with their prize?

GOLD BONE

STICK MAN by Marce

OK

Romans 1:16
I Am Not Ashamed

In the Bible, we read about Saul, a Jewish man who hated Christians. He believed that by hating and hurting Christians he was really loving God! How wrong he was! One day, as Saul was travelling along the Damascus Road on his way to capture more Christians, a great, blinding light appeared. He fell to the ground and heard the mighty voice of Jesus saying "Saul, Saul. Why are you trying to harm me?" After that, something wonderful happened to Saul. He went from enemy of Jesus to friend of Jesus. He became a brave messenger, an apostle. And he got a new name – Paul. Paul once told his Christian friends in Rome "I am not ashamed of the gospel." He meant, "I'll tell anyone anywhere God's good news!" Isn't it wonderful how God changed Saul the murderer into Paul, God's chosen messenger? Will you bravely and boldly stand up for Jesus, like Paul did?

READ THE BIBLE
Romans 1:8-17

SING
'I Am Not Ashamed'

LET'S PRAY!

Lord and God, thank you that you can take your enemies and turn them into your friends through your mighty gospel. Thank you for doing that to Paul, the apostle. Help me not to be ashamed of your powerful, life-changing gospel. Amen.

1 Thessalonians 5:24 'Faithful'

Have you ever seen a car or a truck broken down beside the road? Maybe you were in it! Driving along, then suddenly...clank! Snap! Bump! Grind! The engine stops and there you are, stuck by the side of the road until someone comes to tow the car away or fix it. Things break and let you down don't they? And people can let you down too. They may promise to do something for you but forget to, or tell you a lie, or just can't do it. God isn't at all like the broken car or the promise-breaker. God is The Promise Keeper. When He promises to keep and change and love all who follow Jesus – He will do it! God always keeps His word. He never forgets, never fails, never lies. God never breaks His promise and He never says "Oops! That wasn't meant to happen!" God is ...faithful!

Take Every Thought and Catch It

Have you ever taken a bite of a shiny red, delicious–looking apple only to find that inside it's brown and rotten and horrible? Yuck! Things that look good may not always be good. Jesus said it's not so hard to trick people by looking nice on the outside but to have a hard, unforgiving, unforgiven heart that's far from God. Following Jesus is something you do on the inside, as well as the outside. We have thoughts all the time, don't we? God wants us to catch our bad, selfish, sinful thoughts, own up to them and ask His forgiveness. That's what you do when you confess your sins. God wants our forgiven, clean minds to think about Jesus. Then what's on the inside will show on the outside in a life full of God's goodness and grace.

What doesn't belong in the ZOO? Can you find them?

READ THE BIBLE

SING 'Take Every Thought and Catch It'

LET'S PRAY! Lord and God, I confess my sinful, selfish thoughts to you. I admit I am so often bad on the inside, where only you see. Please forgive me and help me to think about Jesus and obey Him – to live for Jesus, inside and out. Amen.

Fruit of the Spirit

What fruit grows on an apple tree? Apples!
What fruit grows on a mango tree? Mangos! And
what fruit do we get from a peach tree? Yes! Peaches! I
wonder if you have ever seen a strong, healthy tree hanging
with juicy, delicious fruit, ripe and ready to be picked and
enjoyed. God's word says that, like that tree, faithful,
trusting, growing Christians will bear fruit – the fruit that
comes from God's Spirit living and working in them.
It's not the kind of fruit you eat. It's Love, Joy, Peace.
Patience and Kindness. Goodness and Faithfulness.
Gentleness and Self-control. We grow and
show the precious, wonderful, good fruit of
God's Spirit in our life as we say "NO!"
to sin and "YES!" to Jesus, over
and over and over again.

READ THE BIBLE
Galatians 5:22-26

SING ♪ 'Fruit of the Spirit'

LET'S PRAY!

Dear Jesus, you are so good. Please help me to grow and show your Holy Spirit fruit as I live my life in you and for you. Help me to say YES to you and NO to sin over and over and over again. Amen.

Colossians 3:23
Workin' for the Lord not Men

Think of everything you did today. Now think of everything you did last week. Now try and think of everything you've done since your last birthday and the one before and... Woah! That's a lot of stuff to think about! There are big things, exciting things, things we will remember all our lives. And there are lots of little, forgettable, silly, boring, unpleasant things. But here's a tough question: Of all the things you do, which bits do you think God wants you to do for Him? Some of it? Lots of it? No! ALL of it! God owns every moment of your life and He wants you to work at all you do with all your heart – for Him! That's precious and serious and exciting and marvellous all at once! Will you do whatever you do wholeheartedly for God?

READ THE BIBLE Colossians 3:22-24

SING 'Workin' for the Lord Not Men'

LET'S PRAY! Oh God, I do so many things. Some are bad. Please forgive me. Some aren't bad but I sometimes seem to just forget about you while I'm doing them. I pray that you will help me to do whatever I do with all my heart for you. Amen.

Are You Serving Cap'n Jesus

Do you know what a captain does? The captain of a ship is in charge of the whole crew. He decides when and where the ship goes. He gives the order and the crew has to do what he says. And it's his job to look after the ship and everything and everyone on it. When the Bible says "Jesus is the Lord" it means that, like a captain, He is in charge. But not just in charge of a ship – Jesus is in charge of all Creation! In charge of everyone and everything – everywhere! How precious to trust Jesus as your mighty Captain. Through storms and sickness and sadness, He will safely lead His children to their home with Him forever. Jesus is a treasure that can never be lost! So... are you serving Captain Jesus?

FOLLOW THE ROPES
to find out which pirate
is the Captain of
which boat!

ROWENA

NO-NAME

SS SPEEDEE

READ THE BIBLE
Colossians 1:15-20

SING
'Are You Serving
Cap'n Jesus'

LET'S PRAY!

Jesus, you are King of All. I praise you that you made and rule and care for everything. Thank you that as I trust in you I can be sure that you are my kind and strong and faithful Captain. Help me to obey you and treasure you above all else. Amen.

Blessed Be the Name of Jesus

The Bible teaches us that God is a giver. Can you think of some of the good things we treasure and enjoy that come from our good God, the Giver? The Bible also teaches us that God is a taker. He takes away homes, health and comforts. Many times we read of His people who faced hardship, sadness and even death as they faithfully followed Him. Why would God take away good things? Well, we know from God's word that His love endures forever – it never ever stops. So God is always good. We know that He works all things for the good of everyone who loves Him. God is always good to His people. And we know God has a big, beautiful, deep plan to bring everything together under the rule of King Jesus. So be sure of this: no matter what happens, God will never, never take away the BEST THING – Jesus! Blessed be the Name of Jesus!

BIBLE SUFFERERS

They LOVED GOD. They suffered.

DAVID was HATED by KING SAUL. Saul hunted him and wanted David DEAD.

ELIJAH gave up and prayed that he'd just die.

JOB lost everything he owned, lost his family, lost his health.

The LORD gave and the LORD has taken away; may the name of the LORD be praised! JOB 1:21

PAUL was hungry, shipwrecked, thirsty, in rags, bashed up, homeless, hated and hurt for loving Jesus

READ THE BIBLE

SING 'Blessed Be the Name of Jesus'

LET'S PRAY! Oh Lord, help us to trust you as giver of the only everlasting treasure – Jesus. Keep our hearts from trusting in things and people that won't last. Hold us close to you in our times of sadness and sorrow. Thank you for your safe, strong, forever love. Amen.

Here are the words of the songs featured in this book.

Super Saviour

Who can save the day?
Take our sins away?
Who can rescue us
With mighty power…?

CHORUS
Super Saviour
To the rescue!
Super Saviour
Mighty to save!
Look!
Look!
Here comes Jesus
Up! Up!
And out of the grave!

REPEAT CHORUS

He's the death Crusher   *Death Crusher*
Sin Smasher   *Sin Smasher*
Who's the Mighty Super Saviour?
JESUS!

REPEAT CHORUS

1-2-3-4

INSTRUMENTAL

Who can save the day?
Take our sins away?
Who will rescue us
With mighty power…?

CHORUS x 2

Super Saviour (x4)

Words and music by Colin Buchanan
© 2007 Universal Music

Ze Baddest Sickness

1. Well zere's a nasty sickness going round
   It is in ze country unt ze town
   Little babies got it
   Oldies got it, too
   It's vorse zan ze old oomba loomba flu…

CHORUS
Ze baddest sickness in ze vorld is sin
Every single heart has got it in
You got to come to Jesus
He's ze only vun who heals us
Yes ze baddest sickness in ze vorld is sin

2. Zere are times ven sickness go away
   Take ze pills for 8 or 7 day
   But sin is never like that
   It stays inside of you
   And vunce you got it – nothing they
       can do…

BRIDGE
You break ze leg – ow!
Zey do ze plaster
You cut ze hand – yah!
Zey stitch it faster
But sin – Oh goodnessme!
It is ze vorse emergenceeeee!

Only Jesus can relieve it
Hear ze gospel and believe it
You'll be healed if you receive it now….
(Music bit…)

INSTRUMENTAL VERSE

FINAL CHORUS
Ze baddest sickness in ze vorld is sin
Every single heart has got it in
You got to come to Jesus
He's ze only vun who heals us
Yes ze baddest sickness in ze vorld is sin…

CODA
Ze Bible's prognosis
Sin's our diagnosis
Ve're all in zis position
Ve need ze Great Physician
His vonderful salvation
Is our one inoculation
Cos only Jesus Christ can heal
Ze baddest sickness in ze vorld
Zat's sin…

You see?
Vithout Jesus, ve are all fully sick.

Words and music by Colin Buchanan
© 2007 Universal Music

Global Warning

Listen to the GLOBAL WARNING   (echo)
Coming at you and me   (echo)
Jesus' GLOBAL WARNING   (echo)
Repent and believe   (echo)

When you repent you turn around   (echo)
You turn away from sin   (echo)
When you believe in Jesus Christ   (echo)
You put your trust in Him   (echo)
Listen to the GLOBAL WARNING   (echo)
Coming at you and me   (echo)
Jesus' GLOBAL WARNING   (echo)
Is repent and believe   (echo)

When you repent you turn around   (echo)
You turn away from sin   (echo)
When you believe in Jesus Christ   (echo)
You put your trust in Him   (echo)
Birrrrrrup Birrrrrrup Birrrrrrup Bay   (echo)
Booorup Booorup Boo Ro   (echo)
Naa Naa Na Nun Nun Na   (echo)
Wahp Wahp Waa   (echo)

Listen to the GLOBAL WARNING   (echo)
Coming at you and me   (echo)
Jesus' GLOBAL WARNING   (echo)
Is repent and believe   (echo)

Listen to the GLOBAL WARNING   (echo)
Gotta repent   *Repent*
Gotta believe   *Gotta believe*
In Jesus

Words and music by Colin Buchanan
© 2007 Universal Music

Only Jesus Can Make Sin Disappear

1. Have you seen the magic trick guy
   You seen what he can do
   With an abrica ca dabrica
   And a bippety boppety boo
   He'll pull a rabbit from a hat
   And flowers from who knows where
   He's got a special bag of tricks
   And he hides them all in there
   (I s'pose…)

CHORUS
Only Jesus canmake sin disappear
Really truly ruley disappear
There's no secret trick to hide
He did it when he died
Only Jesus canmake sin disappear

2. Well the tricking guy will tell you
   That there's nothing up his sleeve
   Then next thing he's done something
   That you just cannot believe
   But is he really magical
   I tell you he is not
   He's bought a bunch of tricks
   And had to practise them a lot…

REPEAT CHORUS

3. Well it's one thing to have tricks
   That will make you ooo and ahhh
   But all that Jesus did is much more
   Wonderful by far
   He died a suffering Saviour
   And rose again to life
   No tricky smoke and mirrors
   For the mighty Jesus Christ

CHORUS
Only Jesus canmake sin disappear
Really truly ruley disappear
There's no secret trick to hide
He did it when he died
Only Jesus canmake sin disappear
Three days and then
Kazaam!
He rose to life again
Only Jesus can make sin disappear!

Words and music by Colin Buchanan
© 2007 Universal Music

The B-I-B-L-E

CHORUS
God has spoken to YOU AND ME
In the B-I-B-L-E
It's the word of God, you see
The B-I-B-L-E

Better than the TV   *Un Deux Trois*
Better than a movie   *Un Deux Trois*
Better listen carefully   *Un Deux Trois*
To the B-I-B-L-E

CHORUS

Better than the internet   *1-2-3!*
Better than the SMS   *1-2-3*
Better read it every chance you get   *1-2-3*
The B-I-B-L-E

It's God's perfect revelation
By the Spirit's inspiration
It's the story of salvation
For you and me
The B-I-B-L-E…(Bible!)

CHORUS

The B-I-B-L-E (x2)
Hoi!

Words and music by Colin Buchanan
© 2007 Universal Music

From Everlasting (Psalm 90)

From everlasting Woah
To everlasting Woah
You alone are God (x3)

We are like the grass that grows and dies
And death blows clean away
But to you O God a thousand years
Are like a single day…

From everlasting Woah
To everlasting Woah
You alone are God (x3)

You see our every secret sin
Deserving holy wrath
O renew us in the morning with Your
Sweet unfailing love…

From everlasting Woah
To everlasting Woah
You alone are God (x3)
INSTRUMENTAL

From everlasting Woah
To everlasting Woah
You alone are God (x2)

From everlasting
You alone are God
(repeat x 2)

Words and music by Colin Buchanan
© 2007 Universal Music

God Does!

Who sits as heaven's King?   *God does!*
Who cares for everything?   *God does!*
Who brings the rain and snow
Causes the plants to grow
Who makes the wind to blow?   *God does!*
Who does good?   *God does!*
And who saves?   *God does!*
And who alone deserves our praise?
    God does!

Who always says what's right?   *God does!*
Who keeps you safe at night?   *God does!*
Who's full of righteousness
Power and holiness
Who always does what's best?   *God does!*

Who does good?   *God does!*
And who saves?   *God does!*
And who alone deserves our praise?
    God does!

Who sets the guilty free?　God does!
And loves them eternally?　God does!
Who hears their every prayer
Watches them everywhere
Who keeps them in His care?　God does!

Jesus Number 1

CHORUS
Jesus is Number One
Right at the top where He belongs
Who He is and what He's done
Make Jesus Number One
(repeat)

VERSE
He's the Son of God
Jesus Number One – Yeah!
He rose from the dead
Jesus Number One – Yeah!
He'll rule eternally
Jesus Number One – Yeah!
He has supremacy
Jesus Number One…

CHORUS x2

REPEAT VERSE

CHORUS x4

Jesus Number One (x4)

INSTRUMENTAL

Romans 1:16
(I Am Not Ashamed)

CHORUS
I am not ashamed of the gospel
Because it is the power of God
I am not ashamed of the gospel
Because it is the power of God
Power to save everyone who believes
First for the Jew and the Gentile too (yeah)

I am not ashamed of the gospel
Because it is the power of God

INSTRUMENTAL

CHORUS

I am not ashamed of the gospel
Because it is the power of God
Romans 1 verse 16
Romans 1:16
Romans 1 verse 16
Romans 1:16

1 Thessalonians 5:24
(Faithful)

CHORUS
Faithful – Is the God who calls you
Faithful – Is the God who calls
Faithful – Is the God who calls you
And He will do it!
(repeat)

I Thessalonians 5:24 I said that's
I Thessalonians 5:24
Well you know how it says 'He will do it?'
What is it that He will do?
Well everyone He calls
He will…
SAVE them
CHANGE them
KEEP them
HOLD them
Ready for Jesus' return
Ready for Jesus' return

CHORUS x2

I Thessalonians 5:24
I said that's I Thessalonians 5:24
He is FAITHFUL!

Take Every Thought
And Catch It

INSTRUMENTAL

CHORUS
Take every thought and catch it (gotcha)
Chuck out all of that sin (bye bye)
Take every thought and catch it
And think about J-E-S-U-S
And fix your thoughts on Him

1. Gotta chuck out envy
   No room for greed
   Cos God has blessed you
   With all you need… (so)

   CHORUS

2. Gotta chuck out hatred
   And bitterness
   Gotta repent
   Change your mind
   And confess… (and)

   CHORUS

   INSTRUMENTAL

3. Whatever is noble
   Pure and true
   Think on all
   God's done for you… (and)

   CHORUS

The Fruit of the Spirit
of Christ

You know
God's own Son can break the chain
That makes you slave to sin and shame
And when you call on Jesus' Name
You will receive His Spirit

CHORUS
Love, joy peace
Patience and kindness
Love, joy peace
Goodness and faithfulness
Love, joy peace
Gentleness and self-control
This is the fruit of the Spirit of Christ

BRIDGE
Fruit is good and it comes to the life
That is filled with the power
Of the Spirit of Christ
Fruit is good and it comes to the life
That is filled with the power
Of the Spirit of Christ

CHORUS

You know
God's own Son can break the chain
That makes you slave to sin and shame
And when you call on Jesus' Name
You will receive His Spirit
(repeat x 2)

CHORUS (repeat last line x 2)

C'mon now

BRIDGE

Colossians 3:23 (Workin'
For The Lord Not Men)

CHORUS
Whatever you do,
WORK! With all your heart
Like you're working for the Lord, not men
(repeat)

VERSE
Colossians chapter 3
Huh! Hah!
Verse 23, Hah!
Here we go
Hey-oh, Oh-hey-oh
Working for the Lord, not men
We go
Hey-oh, Oh-hey-oh
Working for the Lord, not men

You got to start it all over again…

CHORUS

REPEAT VERSE x 2

Are You Serving
Cap'n Jesus

Arrrr you…
Serving Cap'n Jesus?
(He's the) Master of the wind and waves
There's YO HO HO no other name
By which you can be saved
Through scurvy, shark and shipwreck
In every storm and strife
Sail on with Cap'n Jesus
As the treasure of your life

Climb the rigging!　Aye aye Cap'n!
Swab the deck!　Aye aye Cap'n!
Row the longboat!　Aye aye Cap'n!

And dance the hornpipe now…!

Heave away! Haul away!
Heavy away! Haul away!
Land ho!
Land ho!
Land ho!
LAND HO!

Blessed Be the Name
of Jesus

CHORUS
The Lord gives
The Lord takes away
Blessed be the Name of Jesus
(repeat)

1. We are mist, we are but dust
   Like the grass we wither
   Desperate we call upon
   The mighty mercy-giver

   CHORUS

2. We are poor and destitute
   We cannot win His favour
   And yet He meets our frailty
   With a Spirit-giving Saviour

   CHORUS

3. In wise and holy tenderness
   He has planned your story
   He'll draw His children onwards
   To enfold them in His glory

   CHORUS

   Blessed be the Name (x2)
   Blessed be the Name of Jesus
   Jesus (x4)

These songs are all from my CD, 'Practise Being Godly', which is available separately

John 6:37

Jesus is so mighty! He's called the King of Kings and the Lord of Lords and the Name above every name. Wow! I'm a man now, but when I was a little boy I would ask myself, "If Jesus really is the greatest One of all, can I really know Him? Will He notice me if I pray to Him and ask Him for forgiveness?" One day, when I was a little boy, someone told me about a precious verse from the Bible.

It's where Jesus said, "Whoever comes to me I will never drive away." Can you guess what I did when I heard that? I went straight to Jesus! Even though I was a child, I knew Jesus was telling the truth. God led me to Jesus. I came to Him and He will never drive me away! What a wonderful, mighty Saviour! Will you come to Jesus, too?

READ THE BIBLE
John 6:35-40

SING 'John 6:37'

LET'S PRAY! Oh Jesus, thank you that you are so kind. Thank you that everyone the Father gives you you'll never turn away. Thank you that you are Saviour to big and small, young and old. Amen.